MW01715421

Have a great journey

Mike Maurer

A Journey Through A Warrior's Soul

Perfume River Publications

A Collection of Poems, Drawings, and Photographs

by
Michael P. Maurer

ISBN 0-09720484-2-1

Perfume River Publications
1420 2nd Ave. N., Suite 304
Sauk Rapids, Minnesota, 56379

Edited by Mickey Cunningham and Tracie Kniazkova

Printed in the United States of America by MK Group, St. Cloud, Minnesota

Net proceeds from the sale of this book go towards funding a Vietnam Memorial Scholarship at St. Agnes High School, St. Paul, Minnesota and the Pham Thi Yen Nhi Peace Scholarship at the University Of Science, Hue, Viet Nam.

Dedication

To all our friends who never came home.
May they forgive us.

To warriors, past and present, who
have had to make difficult
life and death decisions and
have had to live with the consequences
of those decisions throughout their lives.

This has been written with the hope that all warriors
may rediscover the spirit of their childhood,
be whole and at peace
with themselves and all peoples.

And for my children and the children of all veterans,
that these writings may help them understand us,
our warrior experiences
and help them forgive us for our shortcomings.

Contents

Part I In Country

Part II Back In the World

Contents

Part III Reflections

Part IV Last Patrol

Part I

In Country

T82

The Journey

On my journey to become a man,
I became something else.

I march along a well-worn path
Traveled by my father, his father
And fathers and sons before them
Throughout time.

I left my youth, my boyhood
On the altar of tribal rituals
In the ceremony of the warrior.

I moved awkwardly through the obstacle course
Challenging my physical limits,
Testing myself,
Pushing myself
To become a soldier, to become a man.

I crawled through the night infiltration course,
Wiggling under the wire
In full combat gear,
My rifle in hand, my brothers beside me
While demented or battle weary DI's fired over our heads,
Reenacting bloody dramas of the past,
Preparing us for the dramas yet to come.

We were practicing the art of war
On the journey
Traveled by so many before us.
We crawled through the blood of our fathers
And our father's memories.

We ran through the bayonet course
Thrusting our rifle before us,
Stabbing our bayonets
Into the complacent dummies
That accepted our repeated attacks without protest;
With each thrust we screamed our mantra.
"The spirit of the bayonet fighter is to kill!"
"The spirit of the bayonet fighter is to kill!"

We conditioned our minds
Even more than we conditioned our bodies.
We emerged as a lethal team

Full of righteous violence,
Full of ourselves,
Ready, waiting to be released
Like attack dogs,
Snarling, pulling at our chains,
Waiting to be unleashed to our destinies.

We wore our uniforms with pride
As inviolate armor
Mounted our steeds,
Charging off to conquer new lands
To slay dragons
And win maidens,

Working to prove our manhood,
Our bravery
As youth had done throughout time.

We had followed the path,
Made the journey
As our fathers expected of us.
Through some mysterious eight week process
Society now saw us as men,
We saw ourselves as heroes
Along with great warriors of the past.
We saw ourselves as invincible, immortal,
As brave beyond belief,
Masking, burying our fears, our doubts
In the bravado of youth
We had become warriors,
Killers some,
Others fodder,
All sacrificial lambs to the call of manhood.

We moved down the path
Unconsciously repeating the mantra.
"The spirit of the bayonet fighter is to kill!"

Even as our lives changed,
As our view of manhood changed,
The mantra repeated itself in the dark recesses of our minds
Coloring our vision,
Our view of the past,
Our view of the future,
Changing the course of our journey.

The Game

I crouched in the shadows
Waiting for the attack,
Anticipating its direction.

I held the pistol tightly,
Waiting, barely breathing,
Knowing I must be still
And quiet to win the game.

He approached me rapidly,
Moving too quickly to be cautious,
Holding his rifle loosely in both hands.

He was only a few feet away
When I stepped out,
Pointed the pistol at his chest
And pulled the trigger repeatedly
Before he realized what had happened.

The caps exploded with each trigger pull.
The red paper with it's burnt charges
Rapidly flowed from the top of the gun.
I kept firing until the roll of caps was nearly spent.

My little brother knowing his part,
Played out his role,
Dramatically falling to the ground,
His small hand clutching his chest,
Wiggling in a prolonged death dance,
Closing his eyes he finally laid still.
I knelt and bent over him,
Putting my cap pistol back
In the plastic holster that hung too loosely
From my narrow hips.

I pushed his toy rifle away
Knowing the game was nearly over
And that mom's cookies awaited us inside.

I checked my little brother's pretend wounds
Assuring myself he was dead,
Before quickly going to his stomach with both hands
Tickling him mercilessly

Until he curled tightly into a ball, laughing uncontrollably;
We rolled over each other repeatedly,
Each trying to tickle the other.

We laughed and laughed until we cried,
Then laid next to each other,
Tears running down our cheeks,
Totally exhausted.

I wiped the tears from my face
As I leaned over him more closely,
Studying his boyish face
And the dark, wet stain that soaked his shirt.
I forced open his still pliable fingers on his right hand
And removed the AK47 from his grip.

I knelt over him, sitting back on my ankles,
Reliving again and again the game we had just played,
As I stared at the lifeless form before me
That only moments ago had been a man
Before my decision to fire.

My fingers loosened on my weapon,
It fell to the ground at my side,
I took off my helmet,
Ran my fingers through my hair in my anguish and cried.

Weeping for the soldier, the boy I had killed.
Weeping for myself and the little boy inside me who had just died.

I thought of my youth
Not much removed.
I thought of the little boy I had been.
I thought of my little brother,
Of all the times we had played the game
When we both walked away
To share mom's cookies
And play the game again.

No one would walk away this time.
I wondered if I could ever eat mom's cookies again
Without crying.

I didn't want to play the game anymore.
Never again.

But the game went on and I was still a player
Trapped in the games of my youth.

Soldier's Spirit

Soldiers then, soldiers still.
We marched together to the warrior's song.
The spirit of the soldier is to kill.

We never thought our blood would spill.
Full of bravado, our bodies strong.
Soldiers then, soldiers still.

We patrolled the jungles and fired at will.
We brought our weapons and our God along.
The spirit of the soldier is to kill.

Screaming, charging up each hill.
The killing just went on so long.
Soldiers then, soldiers still.

I'm unsure of God, but I had my fill.
It all just seemed so terribly wrong.
The spirit of the soldier is to kill.

The deadly images still bring a chill.
And something in my soul seems gone.
Soldiers then, soldiers still.
The spirit of the soldier is to kill.

The Prize

My hand went unconsciously to my neck
As it did so many times each day,
Fingering the gold capped tooth
That hung from the chain.

Remembering the violent time
So long ago
That brought me the prize.

Remembering the man,
The victim,
The corpse
Who had unwillingly awarded the prize.

Remembering a time
Of firefights and victims,
Of killed and killers,
Of terror and rage.

Thinking
Of what I was,
Of what I had become,
Of what I am,
Of the thin line between then and now,
Of the fear of the darkness I found within myself.

We must not forget
Those things we discover
About life,
About death,
About ourselves.

I fingered the prize,
Remembering.

Choices

The choices we make
Sometimes change the course of our lives
Or end it.

He chose wrongly
And died for that choice,
A choice that allowed me to live
At the cost of taking his life.

He was behind me,
I never heard him,
Just the AK47 firing at my back
From a few feet away.

But he chose his target carelessly
With little thought,
He thought he had won,
But with his choice
He lost,
Lost everything.

I wonder if he knew he had only seconds to live?
I wonder if he was as terrified as I was
Or if he was filled with elation,
With a false euphoria,
Believing he had won,
That he had cheated death?

A simple choice,
Three doors,
Three targets,
Only one held a rifle,
Two would be easy,
Unarmed,
Distracted by tending a wounded friend.

The third with the rifle would be easy
Only if he chose them first,
A simple choice,
One you live,
One you may not.

He had us all
If he did it right.

A home run,
A grand slam,
A blowout,
No contest.

I wonder what he saw,
What he felt
In those few seconds he had to decide,
His last seconds.

Perhaps he didn't think,
Excited about so many seemingly easy targets,
Perhaps he just threw the dice,
Pulled the trigger,
Believing there was little to decide,
Just shoot and live
Or don't shoot and die.

But he made the wrong choice,
Chose the wrong door,
Chose the wrong order.
He killed Carrol with his first shots.

Now it was a western shoot out
At three paces.
Was I that fast,
That lucky?
Or was he too slow,
Too slow to move to the next target?
Fascinated,
Captivated watching his bullets dance up Carrol's back?

Rolling to face him
Before he could shift his aim,
Before he could play the same dance on my back,
I fired as I rolled,
Killing him with one shot.
The one shot left in my rifle.

A great shoot-out scene,
Worthy of the best western.
Did the good guy win?
The distinctions unclear.

Did anyone win?
Are we all losers
Just in different ways?

He gave up his chance to kill me
In favor of killing Carrol.
For that choice I killed him.

Was it skill?
Was it luck?
Was it fate?
Was my life any more valuable than his?
Did I live for some greater purpose?
Or was it just the result of the choices we made?

He laid there,
Something different than he had been only moments before.
I walked away,
Also different than I'd been.
He had killed me as I had killed him
Though his death was clearer,
More final.
He died once,
I've died over and over.

Who won?
Who lost?
We both made our choices,
We both died because of them.

Geckos' Commentary

I first heard them in the valley.

We had broken off contact,
Gathered our wounded
And pulled back to a more defensible position
To dig in and try to survive the night.

Dusk settled around us
Almost imperceptively in the darkness of the jungle.

We moved slowly,
Clawing our way back up the trail,
Carrying our wounded and our wounds.
The gunfire had stopped as both sides repositioned themselves.
It was replaced by an eerie stillness.

The first call was distinct and framed by the stillness,
"Fuck you."
It was answered by another to our left, "Fuck you."

They taunted us as we continued to climb,
Calling to us again and again as we dug in on a hill top.

It had taken a few moments to realize that it wasn't the NVA
Taunting and challenging our retreat,
That they too were forced to listen to the ringing commentary that encircled us.

Some of us realized fairly quickly that it was the small lizards,
The geckos which some of us had seen.

They were offering their succinct comment on the war,
On our presence in their jungle.

They sang to us through the night
As we huddled in our holes waiting for an attack.

They sang to the NVA,
To their audaciousness
As they moved down trails on the adjacent mountain,
Their flashlights dancing in a surreal scene.

They called to all of us,
Reminding us of our situation,
Of their long existence in these jungle hills,
Of their persistence before and after us.

“Fuck you.” They sang over and over,
Every time the night fell,
Every time the explosions ended,
Every time the gun fire stopped.

They reminded us of what they thought of the situation,
What they thought of us bringing war to their mountains,
“Fuck you.”

Who's Side Was God On?

If God was on our side,
Who was on theirs?

We each petitioned our God to preserve us and help us destroy the enemy,
But I never saw God on the battlefield,
In our uniform or theirs.

Where was God and who's side was God on?

Did our petitions for courage and safety,
Fall on the same God?
Did God cheer for one side over the other?
Or was God torn like the parent of sons playing for opposing teams?
Did God cheer each side's victories and the souls they awarded?
Did God stand indifferently on the sidelines bored by the action?
Did God laugh at the foolishness of each side asking for divine help to destroy the other?
Did God turn disgustedly and walk away,
Disappointed by our species and our willingness to kill each other in God's name?

Where was God and who's side was God on?

Believing God was on our side,
We raced forward, confident in our righteousness,
Clutching our ideologies, our idealism and our weapons,
Anxious to destroy each other in God's name.

If God was on our side,
Who was on theirs?

Dear John

I showed the letter to Woody.
I just laughed,
We laughed together.

I was beyond crying,
Beyond caring,
Perhaps beyond loving anymore.

The love of my life had written to me in the Nam
To tell me we were through,
That she was going out with someone new
And I didn't care.

I only cared about my brothers,
About the next mission,
My survival
Day to day,
Moment to moment.

"Dear John."
It didn't mean nothing.

My world had contracted to the small space around me,
To the short distance a bullet might travel in the jungle.

I drew no comfort from a distant love.
I drew comfort from my brothers,
I loved my brothers,
The men who fought beside me.

When they died,
I stopped loving anyone,
Maybe even myself.

"Dear John."
It didn't mean nothing.

Fishing With Grenades

The children chattered excitedly,
As more fish floated to the surface.

Some children already held fish,
The shiny, silver prizes were hardly bigger than the tiny hands
That held them.

They tightly clutched their prizes,
Anxious to return home
With their unexpected treasure
That would feed many hungry mouths,
But reluctant to leave,
Hopeful to gain another shiny, silver prize.

The animated chatter of the children
Grew with their expectations.
We couldn't understand their words
But their desire,
Their hope for us to do it again was clear.

We were happy to be able to buy so many smiles so easily,
To share briefly in their joy
At a time when our lives were filled
With fear, violence and sadness.

We threw another grenade
That arched beautifully,
Silhouetted against the morning sky,
The handle falling away,
Igniting the fuse.

We listened to the plop
And watched the splash,
As the grenade fell heavily into the river
Like the countless rocks we'd thrown as kids.

Perhaps for a moment we all thought of those simpler times
Spent by rivers near our homes
With our childhood friends,
Throwing rocks into the depths.

The children cheered
As the muffled explosion faded away

With our memories,
And more fish drifted to the surface.

The explosion disrupted water continued to settle
And an illusion of calm returned to the river,
But not to our minds.

We retrieved the fish,
Passing them out to the children
Who crowded around us
With outreached hands and raised voices
Like children jostling
For the best Halloween treats.

We readied our rifles,
Regaining our game faces
That we'd briefly lost
In those few moments
Of the children's joy and innocence.

We waded in,
Carefully crossing the river,
Continuing our patrol.

We had cleared our path through the water
And were moving on.
We looked ahead trying to anticipate the danger,
Then quickly back at the children
And our memories.

For us, we had merely cleared another river crossing.
To the children,
We were fishing with grenades.

A Simple Gesture

A simple gesture,
A simple gift,
A generosity long remembered,
A meaning much greater than the gift.

An unexpected meeting
On a jungle trail near her home,
I held a rifle,
She held an object
Closed in her hand at her side.

She showed no fear,
I tried to control mine.
My rifle grew increasingly heavy,
My hands tightened their grip
With the tension of the moment
As I tried to read her expression,
To measure the threat.

Was she an enemy,
Or just an innocent civilian too far from her village?
Nothing in her dress or posture gave me a clue.

We held each other's eyes,
I tried to watch her hands,
My fear rising,
A fear of having to act,
A fear of not acting,
Of making the wrong choice,
Of having to live or die with that choice
Trying to weigh the cost of each
In that fraction of a second,
Trying to stay on my feet
Under the crushing weight
Of the decision I had to make,
Knowing that to wait too long
Would be to surrender the choice.

No words were spoken,
No common language to diffuse the moment,
Just our eyes holding each other,
Would these be the last eyes one of us would ever hold?

I tried to discern the object in her hand,
Was it a gun?
A grenade?

My mind raced
Trying to process too much
In too little time,
Trying to make the right decision,
Hoping to make the right decision
For both of us.

I could feel the trigger pressure
Of the M16
I held pointed at her chest.

The trigger pushed back at me
As I pushed on it,
Trying to control,
To measure the pressure.

She started to raise her hand,
Had she killed other GIs,
Taking advantage of their hesitation?
Would I be her victim,
Or she mine?
Which of us was innocent?

What would be worse,
To be killed because I hesitated,
Failed to recognize an enemy threat,
Endangering all behind me?

Or believing there to be a deadly threat
Where there was none,
And carrying the blood of an innocent
On my hands forever?

Would her extending hand offer me life or death?
What would I offer her?

My mind continued its game of ping-pong
At a speed that blurred the ball.
Shoot now while you still can.
No, wait just a second more.
Shoot. No wait. Shoot. No wait. Shoot. No wait. Shoot ....

She dropped the object between us,
The grenade rolled towards me
But instead of running,
She stooped to pick it up,
Extending her hand,
Offering the yam again.

A yam! A potato! Some kind of vegetable!
My God! I'd come so close to killing her,
I'd almost killed her because of a potato,
Because of the setting,
Because of my suspicions,
Because of my fear.

A peace offering
Not a death offering.
Sometimes, some places,
They seem so similar.

I lowered my rifle,
The life draining out of me
With the realization of what I'd almost done.
Not knowing then how that brief moment had changed me,
Not knowing that I'd never be the same,
Not knowing that I'd left some part of me on that jungle trail,
That I gave some part of me to her for what I'd almost done.

The air was different now.
Our fear lifted,
Diffusing through the canopy
Like the jungle steam.

Our fingers touching
With the exchange of the vegetable,
Both of us grateful for the touch,
To be alive to experience the moment.

A simple gesture,
A simple exchange,
A moment of warmth
In a violent and frightening time.

A human connection
Across cultures,
Across languages,
Across time.

More than a vegetable changed hands.
The simple gesture,
The generosity of the gesture
Restored some small measure of hope,
At a time when I'd lost all hope
In humanity,
In cultures,
In governments,
In myself.

A simple gesture,
A small present,
A great gift.

I continued down the trail,
Wondering
What had happened?
What might have happened?
What was different?

Would I be effective anymore?
Would I hesitate too long next time
When the outcome might be different?
Would I get myself or others killed?
Did it matter?

All that mattered in that moment
Was that I'd rediscovered humanity
In a simple gesture.

Killing Ray

I charged him,
Threw myself on him trying to gain the advantage,
Knowing without my rifle it was my only chance.

I hit him hard,
Knocking him backwards to the ground,
Knocking the breath out of him.

My hands quickly gained his throat.
I squeezed with all my might,
Choking the life from him,
Knowing my life depended on it.

I watched his face contort as he struggled
And I squeezed even harder,
Anxious to finish him.

I wanted to live.
I wouldn't let him kill me.

I sensed I was close,
That I had almost won.

Then, suddenly they were all over me,
More than I could count,
Hitting me,
Pulling at my arms and hands,
Beating on me.
Screaming!
"Let him go!"
"Stop it! Damn it!"
"What's wrong with you?"
"You're killing Ray."

Rescued (dustoff)

He saved me,
Saved my life.
Not in the sense you might be thinking
But in a real sense none the less.

At a time when I took a stand,
Committed to a course
To save my soul,
To rescue my spirit,
A course that would have destroyed my life.

He swooped down
Like a dustoff copter into a hot LZ.
He reached out at the last minute
And pulled me up.
He shielded me with his body,
With his reputation.

He risked himself to save me,
So confident in his own strength,
His own power,
Or equally committed to his own course,
His own values,
That he would risk himself,
Risk everything to save me.

He did save me.
He saved me from the war time military machine
That would have ground me up,
Locked me away,
Destroyed my life.

He saved me from a society that sent me to do their killing
But would have rushed to brand me,
To stone me
For my refusal to do
What they would not or could not do themselves.

I had done their killing.
I had given them my body,
Given them my mind.
I had discovered the darkness and wallowed in it.
I had lost my soul,

Lost myself.

I could continue killing,
Continue to destroy my spirit,
My soul,
Myself,
Perhaps forever.

Or I could stop killing,
Refuse to kill again,
Perhaps rescue my spirit,
Perhaps repair my soul,
But lose my life.

I chose to save my soul,
To try to salvage what was left.
I laid down my body,
Offered them my life.

But just when I thought all was lost,
He swooped down
Like a dustoff copter,
He braved the fire,
Absorbed their attacks directed at me,
He stood in front of me,
Extending his arms, his stripes and his reputation,
He shielded me,
He saved me,
Saved me from myself.

I owe him my life.

The Light Show

We sat together
On the roofs of bunkers,
Rifles across our laps,
Shared a beer,
And watched the light show.

Red and green tracer rounds
Raced towards each other
In a deadly game of tag.

Bright flashes of explosions,
Too distant to hear,
Added to the brilliance of the show.

Occasionally,
Green tracers rose into the sky
In vain attempts to find the source
Of the line of red tracers,
That poured from the sky
In a continuous stream of death.

Flares,
Hanging from small parachutes,
Drifted towards earth,
Disappearing as new flares ignited above them,
Creating an eerie mix of illumination and shadows
Across the laser-like show of red and green.

And we watched,
And drank,
And laughed
Mesmerized by the light show,
Too distant or too numb
To think of the deadly drama being played out,
Thankful not to be involved in the action.

For now,
We were happy just to be able to watch the light show.

Enemy Killed: 1714
US Casualties
Killed 119
Wounded 261

Numbers

It was a war of numbers,
Ours against theirs.

It was a numbers game,
Measured by the public's acceptance
Or discomfort with the numbers.

The numbers were closely managed and controlled
By politicians, generals, lower level officers and officials.

They changed the numbers when it was necessary for a better effect,
The numbers were massaged and managed at each level,
Until no one really knew what the real numbers were,
But they knew they liked the final number they wrote down,
They offered them to us with smiling faces
Like slick salesmen
Awaiting our approval.

It was a war of numbers,
Of troop call ups and deployments,
Troop strengths and enemy strengths,
Of casualties, theirs and ours,
Killed In Action,
Wounded In Action,
And body counts,
Of missions flown and bombs dropped.

The numbers were fed to us antiseptically each evening
On the nightly news like some crazy math problem or lottery game.
The numbers were clean and crisp in nice graphic displays,
They looked good,
They were the best numbers experts could create.

The chaos, the horror, the tragedies,
The blood and the fear,
The torn bodies and broken lives had been cleaned away
To make the numbers palatable,
So they could be swallowed easily with our evening suppers
As we sat around our TV,
Removed from the violence.

We would continue to swallow the numbers,
Going about our lives as long as the numbers were shelled and cleaned,
Picked and polished and presented in an appetizing manner.

And so at every level
Everyone worked
To clean up the numbers,
To remove the mud and blood,
To provide clean attractive packaging
Like the supermarket steak
Far removed from the dying animal or bloody carcass that made it possible.

The numbers were garnished with noble phrases
Like "protecting freedom," "ensuring democracy" and "stopping Communist aggressors,"
To make them go down better.

And so we were fed and ate the numbers
Until we were finally full,
And they could no longer hide the bloody carcass while feeding us the steak,
And the garnishes became hollow words that were hard to swallow.

It was a numbers game to the end.

May
Sun Mon

Numbers II

While generals and politicians had their numbers games,
We each had our own game of numbers.

Losing lottery numbers
Became "In Country" calendars.

We memorized DEROS dates
And kept "short timers" calendars,
Checking off each day,
Counting the days till we'd go home,
Back to the world.

We walked carefully,
Exhaustedly through each day,
Checking off the day the next morning
In celebration of surviving the night.

We hoped and prayed to make it through our calendar
Before our number was up,
And we would be added to the casualty numbers
That the generals and politicians tried to manage.

We counted ammunition and grenades,
Hoping we could carry enough
To keep ourselves from becoming just another number
In a plastic body bag,
All the time counting days.

We counted our casualties,
As we laid them in rows
To await medical evacuation
Or the trip to graves registration.

We counted their bodies,
Then multiplied it by some factor of ten
To account for those we missed or that were carried away
And to make the numbers sound better in the face of our losses.

We counted our friends
Until they or we were gone,
Then we battled alone no matter the number around us.

We wore numbers on our backs,
Unseen and unspoken
By us or those around us
But we each knew it was there.

We carried it in the rice paddies,
Along jungle trails,
Trying to win the life and death lottery
We were forced to play.

Some of us won.
Some of us lost.

Those of us who won continued to count the days,
Noting each passing
As another survived.

Waiting for the next sunrise,
Clinging fearfully to the night,
Trying to make another day,
Still keeping our calendar,
Still trapped in a game of numbers.

Part II

Back In The World

Coming Home

It wasn't the parades I missed
Or any welcoming celebrations,
That's not what could have saved me.

For I was hurt,
My soul bled from the darkness I had seen,
From the darkness I had become.

And my heart ached with the sadness of the losses,
The loss of friends,
The loss of youth,
The loss of innocence,
The loss of self.

I didn't need a parade.
I needed to be held
As a parent holds a child
Tightly to their breast to comfort them
After they're rejected by a playmate,
Lose an athletic competition,
Or break up with their first love.

I needed to be comforted in that same manner,
To be held to the breast of my country while I cried,
To have my head stroked and my back patted,
To be told it was alright.

To be held in a loving and cleansing embrace,
To be taken back into the human community,
To be forgiven and loved despite what I had seen,
Despite what I had done,
Despite what I had discovered about humanity,
About myself.

Instead I was left to wander by myself
In my hurt and my confusion
Until I became so lost no one could find me.

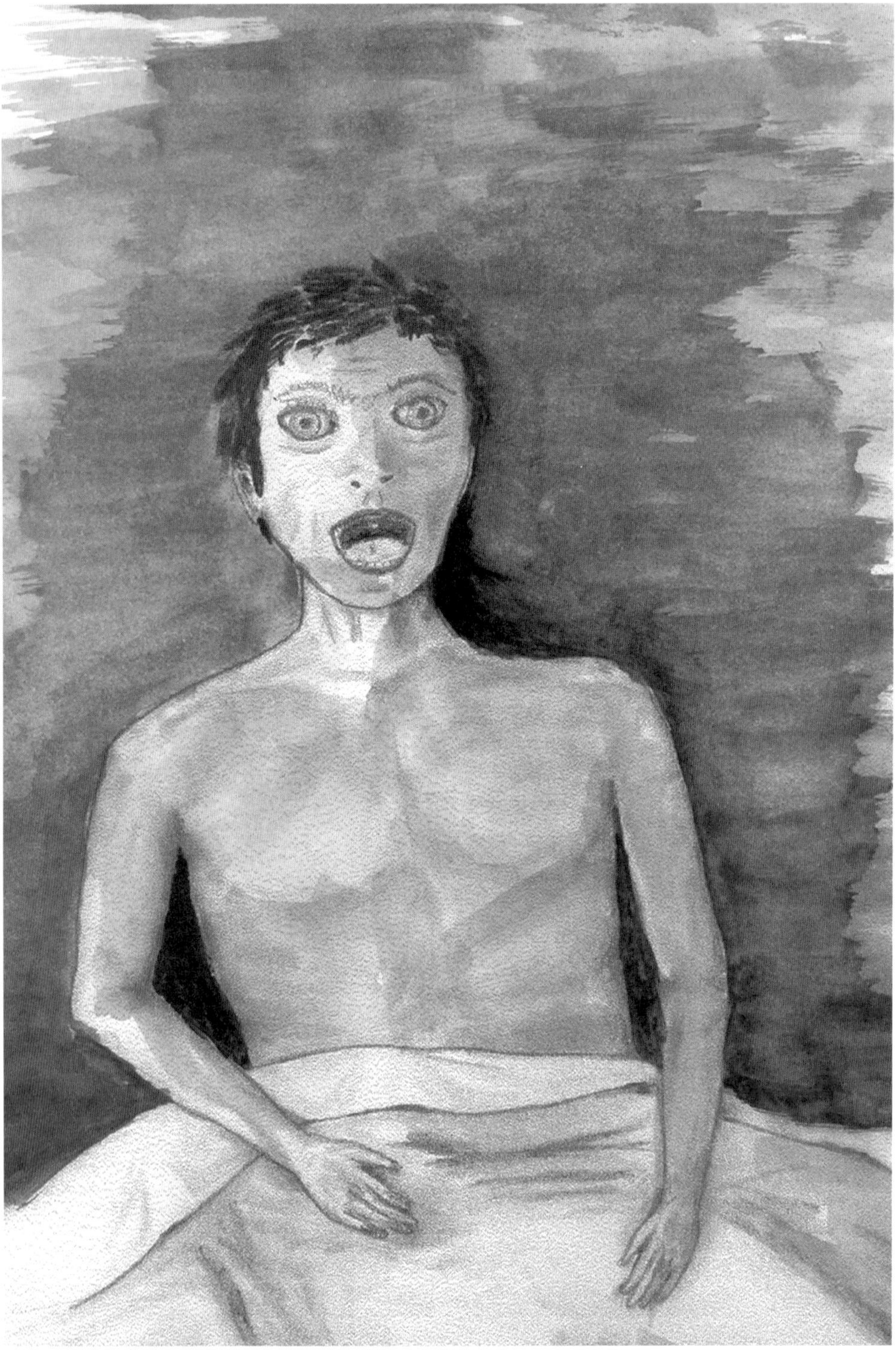

Night Terrors

Medic! I'm hit! Medic!

The terror races from my mouth with my screams,
God don't let me die here.

Gunfire roars in my ears,
Creating a constant din,
Explosions swallow my cries.

Medic! I'm hit! Medic!

I can't move,
I am afraid to move,
I lay frozen in my above ground grave.

Why isn't anyone coming for me?
Where is the rest of the patrol?

I can feel my life draining away,
I scream again with all my remaining strength,
with all my terror.

Medic! I'm hit! Medic!

My terror and my aloneness consume me,
Don't let me die like this.

The jungle is closed in around me,
Concealing the sky, the sun, the light,
Blotting out all hope.

Despite the din of gunfire,
I can hear enemy soldiers crawling all around me,
Oh God, this is the end.

I scream again,
With even more terror than before,
With even more desperation,
Or did I only think I screamed?

Medic! I'm hit! Medic!

The crawling sounds of enemy soldiers grow closer,
My terror overwhelms me,
Closing off the outside world,
Leaving me even more alone, more afraid,
God don't leave me here.

The silence is deafening,
All I can hear are my screams
Echoing in the emptiness
As I race my fears,
And try to outrun my death.

If only I could touch a friend,
See a face,
See the sun,
God, don't let me die like this.

Medic! I'm hit! Medic!

Suddenly, I'm sitting up in my bed,
Screaming at the walls,
Alone with my terror.

Dying

Have you ever thought about dying?
I have,
As I walked through the jungles
Of the Annimite mountains.

I carried my life on my back,
It was a fragile time,
A simple time,
Defined by survival,
By death,
You lived or you died
In simple, violent terms.

I could not die,
I would not die in the jungles,
In that darkness,
Lying on my back,
Suffocating from the dark green cathedral
That oppressed me,
Offering no sun light,
No hope,
Now or then.

But in the fields,
In the paddies,
I could die.

Where I could lay on my back
In my final moments,
Looking at the sun,
Warmed by it,
Welcomed by it.

It made it possible to die,
Perhaps even compelling,
Welcoming,
And so I did.

Lying back,
Clutching my wounds,
My hands wet,
Warm with my blood,
Or the sun,
Or both.

I drank in the sunlight,
It comforted me,
The noise of the battle faded,
All I saw was the sun,
The sun of my youth,
Of happy memories,
The sun drew me to it,
Carried me away.

I could die in the sunlight,
And I did.

My Rifle

There was such relief
That I only needed one shot,
Because that was all there was,
Such a thin thread between living and dying.

I loved my rifle in that moment,
More than anything else,
Even damaged as it was
With the shot that had exploded through the forearm,
It still fired and saved my life.

One shot,
A brief moment
Decided which one of us would live,
And which would die.

I clutched my rifle to my chest,
Holding it in a tight embrace
As one would hold a lover,
Never to let them go.

I still love my rifle,
Embracing it every night
In a comforting reunion of lost lovers
With a shared intimate past.

Hidden Wounds

Waking up I knew I was about to die.
She stood over me,
An AK in her hands.

I crawled backwards,
Frantically groping blindly behind me for my rifle,
Unable to look,
Not daring to let my eyes leave hers,
Muttering or moaning to myself
In my desperation and my fear.

Damn it! Where was my rifle?
I searched desperately, blindly
While I waited for her to fire
And end my life.

Then, inexplicably she turned and ran,
Yelling "Mom, what's wrong with Mike?"

I didn't understand, so I continued to search for my rifle,
Knowing she would be back.

Already Dead

I wander in this wasteland,
Searching for myself.
Sometimes I can be so elusive.

Do I search with purpose,
Or merely to avoid myself?
For the reflections in the mirror of self-examination,
Can be frightening.

It is so frustrating to be so lost,
To wander where there are no paths,
Where the directions are unclear,
And the choices overwhelming.

Is it I that does the seeking,
Or am I chased by the ghosts of past lives
That seek to embrace me
And swallow me whole?

I flounder against the ocean of sadness
That seeks to drown me,
And fight the anger
That threatens to steal my soul.

Is it the deaths that haunt me,
Or the killer I'd become?
When successful as a soldier,
Do we fail as a man?

Is it the inner-self I killed
That perhaps I really seek?
But there is no remaking
Of the self that we destroy.

Am I doomed to wander
In this wasteland ever lost?
Is the platoon out searching,
Or did I alone survive?

Is this really survival,
Or just an illusion
Of those that refuse to die?

Do my victims, my friends and my failures,
Watch with some amusement
And cheer for me to join them?

I continue searching,
Afraid of never finding,
Of always being lost.

But more terrified of finding
A darkness that is me,
And that I'm already dead.

1975

The Dance

Long ago,
I learned the deadly dance
Of rifles and grenades.

I entwined myself
With the mistress of the ball,
Reluctant, fearful at first,
But then willing, even anxious for her embrace.

She held me close,
Closer with each dance
Until I couldn't live without her.

Her power and voice embraced me,
Never to let me go,
I am drunk on her perfume
Of gunpowder, blood and fear.

She is the mistress of my dreams,
Calling to me seductively,
Calling me back to her.

But even as I love her,
Her ugliness surrounds me
And she repulses me,
Even as I am drawn to her.

I love her,
And I miss her,
Even as I hate myself for loving her.

Her voice and smells
Are always with me,
I can't wash her perfume
From my senses or my hands.

She has held me to her warmth,
I have tasted the sweet sickness of her lips and soul,
No other will ever satisfy me.

And thus I dream of my mistress,
Replaying each embrace,
Trying to recapture the feeling,
The beat of the music,
And the magic of the dance.

Under The Radar

He's around
But not really noticeable.

Avoiding crowds
And public places,
Unconsciously practicing the trade from long ago,
Patrolling, hiding, watching.

Living,
Existing alone,
Living on the fringes of society,
Never really in it.

Seldom ever really seen
Like a ghostly image that fades in and out.

All his energy spent
On trying not to be a target,
Trying to survive,
To stay under the radar.

Rain

My fear rose
With the rising billows of dark clouds.

The shadows,
The darkening clouds
Bring a sense of sadness
That closes over me like a veil,
Darkening my soul
Like the clouds themselves.

I envy those who delight in the rain,
Cheering the approaching clouds
With a sense of eagerness,
Anticipating the fresh smell of new rain,
The quiet sounds of the first drops
And the soft wetness on their skin.

But for me,
The approaching clouds
Bring a rising sense of dread,
As though the dark billows
Carry some part of the darkness from my past
That threatens to envelop me.

The first drops of rain
Assail my senses
With the smells of dead and decaying jungle vegetation,
And the smells of death.

There is a rising sense of panic
As I search for an escape,
Not from the rain itself,
But from the memories,
From the fear,
From the sadness
That wash over me with each drop.

I need to run,
But where?
Where is it safe from the rain?
From myself?

The drops fall faster now,
Each drop adds to my panic
That increases with the rising intensity of the rain.

I try to run
And strain to hear at the same time,
Trying to strike some critical balance
Between movement and perception.

The sounds of the rainfall
Overwhelm all other sounds,
Muffling the sounds of death's approach,
Allowing it to sneak up on you unannounced,
Embracing you in its deadly grip
Before you even know it's there.

I know death stalks me in the rain.
I strain to hear it coming
Amid the deafening drops.

Bunkered In

The telephone went unanswered,
The door was securely locked,
Having been repeatedly checked,
Warning devices, in lieu of trip flares, were set,
Rations for a long stay were stacked in the cupboard.

He moved cautiously from window to window,
Careful not to silhouette himself or otherwise offer a target,
He ran his interior patrol,
Checking each lock,
And standing motionlessly watching each approach
Until he was certain there was no one.

He was in a defensive posture,
Prepared for a long stay,
He never knew how long it would be before the terror subsided,
And he could move around again cautiously in the outside world.

Today the terror hung over him, encircled him
Like a dense fog on a cool morning,
And he couldn't escape it or push his way clear.

He knew terror,
Sometimes he still heard them crawling towards him,
Pushing their AK47s ahead of them as they crawled,
Sometimes it was not so much that he heard them as he could feel their presence,
The way you feel someone staring at your back from across a room,
It was a feeling that had kept him alive and he trusted it.

He knew terror,
He had been with the others when they were killed,
He had been tumbled about again and again
By the sudden explosions of violence,
He still heard the screams against the backdrop of the roar of gunfire.

Sometimes the terror overwhelmed him,
Filling his nights
And his days,
All his senses were on edge,
Alert for the attack that always came.

He’d learned
The best way to survive these attacks was to be dug in,
To limit your vulnerability,
To defend from fortified positions.

And so he retreated to this space,
His firebase,
His bunker,
Where no one got in and no one got out,
Where he felt somewhat safe,
As safe as he could at these times.

He was hunkered down,
Bunkered in.

He was careful not to offer any clue to his position
That would make an attack easier,
He’d just quietly hold his ground
Like he always did.

He was hunkered down.
He was bunkered in.

The Beast

Rage,
I don't want to know it anymore.

For rage is an ugly beast
That fueled the fires of my destroying other men.

Vengeance was my purpose,
Resurrection of the dead my goal.

The beast powered me,
It gave me purpose.

I discovered the beast within me,
And I am afraid.

It stalks me,
Taunting my fear.

Rage is an ugly beast,
It fueled the fires that destroyed me.

I am the keeper of the beast,
And the beast is me.

Rage is an ugly beast,
It fuels the fires of my greatest terror.

I have held the beast,
And the beast has held me.

It will always haunt me,
It is always there, on the edges of my terror.

Rage,
I don't want to know it anymore.

Video Library

I have an extensive library of video tapes
Stored in my head,
Recorded in the jungles and rice paddies
Long ago on a distant stage.

The actors are all young,
Boys playing the parts of men,
Most new to their part,
Though they've rehearsed a lifetime.

The action is realistic,
Actors fall, never to rise and play again,
For many it is their first and last part,
But I have the tapes of their final performance.

The tapes have a life of their own,
Replaying continuously
In some kind of unpredictable,
But chilling fashion toward some unknown end.

The clarity of every tape
Remains piercingly sharp,
Despite the millions of times they've been replayed.

The screams are as heart-wrenching,
And as terror-filled as the day they were recorded.
The blood smells as fresh.
The fear tastes as bitter.

Sometimes I unwillingly join in the action.
Even now acting out my part again,
From the original presentation.

While all the banners have long since faded
And the crowds have gone away,
For me the theater remains
In all its opening-night glory.

Innocent cues immediately transport me back
To the horror of the original production,
And the tape replays,
The outcome predetermined.

Now, I stand alone on the stage,
Doomed to repeat my part again and again,
To some unknown director's silent cue.

Despite my exhaustion,
The director compels me to replay the scene
Until I get it right.

Beach Balls

As if holding a beach ball underwater,
I held my Vietnam memories beneath the surface,
Working, straining to hide them from sight,
From myself and from others
So that I would appear normal above the waterline.

It was easy at first.
I was young and strong,
But it became more difficult with each passing day,
With each passing year,
Until finally my arms gave out.

The ball sprang from the water,
Bursting, it released all its stale air and festering memories,
Staining all of us with the explosion.

Music

The sound of the rotors still sings to me.

The song of my youth,
Of assaults and of rescues,
Of friendships and love,
Of the fear, the excitement and the energy
When I was young.

The music calls to me,
Causing me to stop and stare skyward,
Waiting expectantly for the bird to pick me up
And carry away my body as it already has my mind.

I see myself riding, through blue cloudless skies
On hot, muggy days,
The warm wind washing over me,
My feet dangling precariously over the edge,
The music of the rotors loud in my ears,
My friends crowded in next to me
Listening to the same music.
Occasionally we exchange glances,
Reassuring each other of our presence,
But each of us lost in the ride,
And the sound,
And the emotion of the music.

Riptides

Sometimes you decide to wade into the ocean from unfamiliar beaches,
Unaware of the dangerous currents.

That decision unknowingly becomes your last voluntary act,
For the riptides catch you
And carry you along like the events in your life.

Such were the events of Vietnam,
For the nation,
And for each of us
As individuals and as soldiers.

Once we volunteered or submitted to the draft,
We were carried by the riptides
Of the military
And of war.

Each of us were tossed and beaten as we struggled against the current of events
That we were powerless to control or understand,
And powerless to extricate ourselves from.

Some of us drowned,
Others were carried long distances and cast up in strange places,
Exhausted from the struggle,
Never able to re-orientate to the strange world
In which we found ourselves.

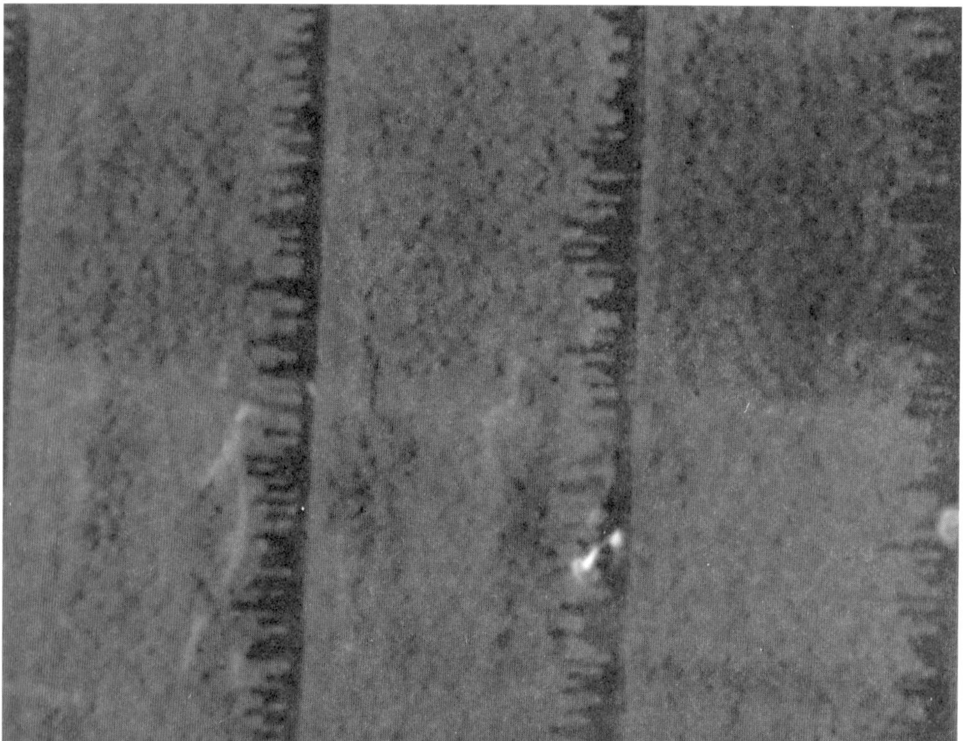

Part III

Reflections

Only Me

I scanned the crowd,
Searching each face,
Wondering,
Hoping that they might be the one,
The one who would save me.

Save me from this pain,
From this sadness,
From this emptiness,
From this confusion,
From my struggle.

Wondering
If they might be the one
Who would dive in,
Brave the depths,
Release my chains,
Pull me up from the bottom,
Breathe new life into my soul.

The crowd passes,
No one stops,
They are unaware of my plight,
Or unable or unwilling to help.

I reach out,
Extending my arms,
Beseeching each person,
But my message is garbled from this depth,
My voice lost in the static,
The chaos of the world.

Then I am alone, again,
By myself.

It is all an illusion,
A fantasy,
A bit of self deception,
Slight of hand.

There is no one,
Will be no one,
No one is coming,

No ambulance,
No rescue squad,
No medic,
Not even a good Samaritan.

There is only me,
Moving ghost-like through the images of my mind.

Only me.

Slackman

With a good slackman you can face anything,
That's what made it possible again and again
To walk the point.

A good slackman made it possible to lead off,
Seemingly fearlessly,
Down jungle trails,
Through paddies and hedgerows,
Into the face of faceless enemies set on destroying you,
Confident that a few steps behind you,
Your slackman had you covered,
Protecting your back,
Ready to catch and hold you
As you tumbled backwards,
Carried by a cascade of events that were out of control.

A good slackman made it possible
To move deliberately forward,
Towards certain tragedy
And the waiting arms of death
That spread out in front of you anxious to embrace you.

How I could use a good slackman these days,
Maybe I could move forward again,
Less cautiously,
Less fearfully,
But good slackmen are hard to find.

Top

I think of him often,
Humping up and down our column
With his rifle and his pack,
Checking,
Always checking.

He was a career soldier
With the highest enlisted rank,
We were mostly privates,
He was the top.

A paratrooper,
An infantryman,
As we were.
He stood tall and proud
And ramrod straight,
Even under the weight of his pack,
His gear,
His responsibility for our lives,
Our safety.

This was our war,
Likely our one and only,
He had served in others,
And likely would serve in more.

He was nearly twice my age,
Twice the age of most of the men he was responsible for,
Though he was directed by officers half his age,
With less than a fraction of his experience.

We were in our prime,
He'd seemingly never left his,
He was tough,
Tougher than most of us could ever hope to be.

He never tired
Or at least never showed it
Like the rest of us did.

He moved up and down our ranks,
Humping twice the distance the rest of us humped,
Checking,

Always checking,
In his tireless, but hopeless efforts to keep us safe.

He was our father,
Our mother,
Our mentor,
Our counselor,
Our protector.

A tough taskmaster,
But a loving parent
Who was always there.

He directed us,
Guided us,
Tried to keep us safe
Like a shepherd herding their flock
Of young lambs
Through a hostile terrain.

We sought his company,
His presence,
We gathered around him,
We drew comfort and courage
From his strength,
His presence.

He was steady,
Unflappable in battle,
Always moving toward the action,
Braver than a man had any right to be.

He shielded us from the enemy,
From our inexperience,
From our youthful belief in our immortality.

He buffered us from officers,
Protecting us from their inexperience
Or their arrogance,
Or both.

He tried to protect us from the system,
From the policies,
The decisions
That endangered us,
That threatened to destroy us all.

But despite his strength,
His experience,
His constant vigilance,
We still died.

He mourned each loss,
Secretly carrying the pain and the sadness,
Always exhibiting the strength we relied on.

With each loss
He redoubled his efforts,
His resolve
To keep us safe,
Moving up and down the column,
Checking on each of us,
Always checking.

The List

We sat quietly together,
Such different people
With a common past.

A retired career soldier
With the highest enlisted rank
Who knew me,
Led me
When I was just a boy,
But a soldier none the less.

We sat quietly together,
Lost in our own reflections
Of the intense and violent time
That created an intimate and permanent bond.

Our shared past,
Our common pain
Had brought us to this memorial,
To this chance meeting
That overwhelmed us both
With memories of our time together,
Eighteen years before.

We sat quietly together,
Lost in the same time,
The same thoughts.

Without explanation,
He opened his wallet
And extracted a tattered piece of paper,
With handwritten names.

He quietly read each name,
Talked about each person,
Their lives,
Their deaths.

Mourned each loss
As if they were each his son,
Who he loved and cherished,
Then and now.

He mourned his inability to keep them safe,
To bring each of them home,
To return each to the loving embrace
Of their real parents.

His guilt and sadness
Hung heavy in the air,
A thick, humid, sauna-like presence
That made it difficult to breathe.
We both struggled for every breath.

I wanted to run,
To escape,
To escape from him,
From the thick air,
From the list,
From my memories,
But I couldn't move.

Instead, I listened quietly,
Respectfully,
To each name,
To each life,
To each death,
Though I knew it all,
Knew each man,
We shared their lives
And their deaths,
They were his men,
His sons,
My friends,
My brothers.

He read them all,
Reviewed each life,
Seemingly lost in himself
As though unaware of my presence,
Or that my presence wasn't necessary,
He reviewed the names for himself
Not for me.

He talked about each person
With such great sadness
As a parent who had lost their children,
So many children,
So much violence,
So much pain.

His pain seemed so great,
It overshadowed my own.

The list showed its own pain
Of countless foldings
And unfoldings,
Of countless handlings,
Of countless tears.

He fingered the list lovingly
As though it were some precious heirloom,
As though to touch the list,
To touch the names
Was to touch the lives again.

I wondered how many times
He had extracted the list,
Held the names,
Reviewed the lives.

And how many more times
He would review the list.

Kirkland's Smile

Kirkland smiled at me
In a permanent grin,
His teeth glistening
Despite the lack of sun.

That moment forever frozen in my mind
Despite the noise and chaos around me,
Despite my preoccupation with survival,
I see Kirkland smiling.

It was a death smile.
Kirkland's last.

How I loved his smile.
How it warmed and comforted me,
For brief moments erasing the fear
That was so constant.

His teeth shined
As though freshly scrubbed.
They probably were.

He was always brushing his teeth.
If we stopped on patrol,
He'd brush his teeth.
Before he went on ambush,
He'd brush his teeth,
He wouldn't need to anymore.

I teased him,
Asking him who he thought he might meet on an ambush,
Or telling him that the NVA didn't care
Whether he had clean teeth or not,
Or that his smile was so bright,
It would make a perfect target.

He said his teeth got fucked up
On his first tour in the Nam,
And he wasn't going to let that happen
On his second tour,
Then he'd smile,
And go brush his teeth.

Kirkland smiled throughout the battle
As though he found some pleasure
In being able to just watch the deathly drama.

I still see Kirkland smiling at me everyday.

The New Guy

I can't remember his name.
That's a lie,
I never knew it.

I never knew him.
I didn't want to know him,
I didn't want to know one more guy,
I already carried too many names.

He was always just the new guy
Even when we patroled together,
Shared a foxhole
Or fought side by side.

He was always just the new guy,
Just another new face
That I didn't want to know,
Didn't want to carry,
However briefly.

It made it easier to carry his body to the helicopter.

But I ended up carrying his face anyway.
Now I wish I knew his name.

The Debt

Sometimes I wonder why I'm still alive.
Okay,
I wonder every day.

Was it simply chance?
Fate?
Dumb luck?
Or was my life somehow more important?
Is it more important than the others?
Am I to do something important?
Something special?

How do you pay for your survival?
Pay back the debt?
A debt to those who died because of you,
Or in your place.

Brocker died because he carried the platoon radio,
The long antenna waving over his head,
Taunting the enemy to try to kill him
And disrupt our communications.

He died carrying the radio
That until that morning I had carried,
He carried the radio I gave him,
Making him trade places with me,
Taking the target from my back
I put it on his,
I handed him his death
And strapped it to his back.

What compelled me to request, to make that change?
It doesn't matter why,
It only matters that I did it
And that Brocker died instead of me.

How could anyone have known
How death was stalking us?
Following us through recent days,
Waiting for the right moment,
Waiting for that morning,
When she embraced us,
Held us tightly,

Breathing her hot, putrid breath in our faces
Until we succumbed
Or were forever changed by the stench.

Kirkland died alone,
Without me,
Without help,
Without hope,
Without goodbyes.

Despite our promises to each other,
Somehow we got separated
Only to be rejoined later
When it was too late,
Too late for Kirkland,
Too late for both of us.

The ensuing battle never allowed time to hold him,
To cry,
To say goodbye,
To tell him I was sorry,
That I didn't know what happened,
All I know is that I can never make it up to him,
Or to myself.

Why am I alive?
Why did I live?
What should I be doing to repay the debt?
To honor the price?
To soothe the guilt?
A burning guilt so deep, so complete
That no treatment,
No ointment,
No cool gauze,
No skin grafts offer relief.

Doc,
Doc Payne, my friend, died early in the battle
Though I didn't know it.

We were buddies,
The kind that only the immediate threat of death can bring,
We repeatedly promised to look after each other,
Promising to save the other,
To keep each other alive especially when hit.

So committed to that cause,
We promised to put a compress on the other's chest
Before the bullet could get out the back,
Impossible to do,
But it emphasized our commitment to saving each other.

Can you envision it?
Can you understand that kind of commitment
To another person in a life and death situation?

We were brothers,
And we made promises to each other,
Backed with the false bravado of our youth.

It was what kept us going,
Walking trails,
Assaulting ambushes,
Charging blindly again and again into enemy positions,
Knowing that we were with our brothers,
That no matter how bad it was,
No matter how no one else seemed to care,
Or nothing else seemed to matter,
We were with our brothers.
They would look after us,
We would keep each other alive no matter what,
No matter what!
We would never leave a brother alone!
Or behind!
And so we continued on,
Knowing that someone with us cared.

I needed Doc now.
Everyone was dying.
I couldn't help them and fight at the same time,
I called for him,
Screamed for him,
And screamed for him again,
First generically "Medic!"
Then by name.

I cursed him
For his abandonment,
For not being there,
For breaking our promise,
But perhaps it was me that abandoned him,

Cursing him as he lay dead unable to come to me,
Perhaps he was killed trying to reach me,
Trying to respond to my screams.

I wondered if he was calling for me
As he lay dying,
If he wondered where I was,
If he cursed me for abandoning him,
For breaking my promise.

So many losses.
So many failures in such a short time.

Carrol died
Because they chose him instead of me.
He died because they got past me,
Got behind me
And chose his back instead of mine.
He was counting on me to keep him safe,
To cover him.

I was a fraction of a second too late ,
A lifetime too late,
Carrol's lifetime.
The AK still exploding in my ears
As I rolled to cover my back,
Extracting a vengeance
That must have been meaningless to Carrol.
They paid for my anger at my failure
But Carrol remained dead.

I was dead but alive,
A poor second choice,
Winning because I wasn't chosen first,
Winning or losing in the lottery of death
Depending on your view.

I've replayed those moments a million times,
The picture is clear,
But there is no clarity,
No understanding ,
No answer
As to why I am alive and everyone else is dead.

Tommy Ray got hit
Standing next to me,
Quietly talking,
He got hit when we were sprayed with AK fire.

I don't recall what he was saying to me,
But I'll never forget his screams
As I laid on top of him,
Trying to burrow both of us into the ground
To avoid the continuing fire.

I can still see the small white marks in his brown flesh
Where the bullet pierced his neck.

I walked away unscathed,
Well at least not bleeding,
All my wounds were internal,
I could feel the blood seeping from my organs,
Draining the life from me,
From the repeated piercing
Caused by each new event.

There were no bandages for my wounds,
No medic rushed to investigate my screams,
Maybe they couldn't hear me,
Maybe only I could hear my screams.

And so
Brocker, Kirkland, Payne, Carrol, and Tommy Ray
Went home,
First in bags, then in boxes,
Riding helicopters then planes.

I went on more patrols,
More ambushes,
To the next valley,
The next hill,
The next battle.

Collecting my invisible wounds,
Walking across the countryside
Step by step,
Inch by inch,
Battle by battle,
Body by body,

Dripping my blood,
My life,
Across the countryside.

Woodson got hit behind me
When they opened up in front of me
Catching us in their ambush.

He screamed for me to help him,
Then screamed for me to stop,
As machine gun fire directed at me
Raked across us threatening to hit Woodson again.

And so we hung there, unable to move,
Suspended somewhere between life and death
Like circus aerialists
Hanging from the wire by their fingertips after a slip.

Only a thread,
A moment separated us from death,
And we dangled by that threat
For what seemed like an eternity,
Afraid to move,
Knowing that if we moved we would die,
But knowing if we stayed we were already dead.

We hung there,
The tension thick like a mountain fog,
Until the wire broke
And we came crashing down.

Woodson went home,
I stayed,
Moving on to new ground,
Or old ground,
It all looked the same,
It was all wet with our blood.

Fraiser died just in front of me,
In my place, stopping me on my patrol
Mere feet in front of hidden enemy positions,
Insisting on taking the point,
He proceeded ahead,
Commanding that I follow him,
That he would show me the way.

He died sprawled across the enemy bunker,
A few feet from where he stopped me to talk
And change positions.

Why they let us stand and talk
And passed up an opportunity to easily kill us both,
I don't know,
As I don't know so many things.

I still don't understand,
Despite the years of reflection,
Of dissecting each encounter,
Each incident of death and survival.

I continue to question my survival.
Had the choice been mine?
Or theirs?
Was it some kind of twisted divine plan?
Or simply chaos and chance?

I seemed to be surviving
On the lives and deaths of friends,
And enemies,
Walking across the expansive, boiling cauldron of blood
On the backs of my friends,
Who floated face down
Offering themselves,
Even if reluctantly,
That I might pass
Without getting my feet wet,
Or my boots bloody.

But the blood was all around me,
Soaking my clothes,
Soaking into my being
To meet my own blood that was seeping out
Through every pore,
Creating some kind of caustic mixture
That would slowly consume me,
Eating me up little by little
Like a torturously slow cancer,
Assuring me of a lingering painful death.

Passavanti was the last
To lay his body down that I might walk across it.

Well, he wasn't really the last,
But he was the last I allowed myself to record,
My pack was full,
I couldn't carry any more bodies,
Any more names,
The rest would have to lay nameless
Where they fell,
Along the trails,
In the jungle,
In the valleys,
On the hill tops,
In the rice paddies.

They continued to fall,
To pile up around me
But I took no notice,
My eyes were shut,
Squeezed tightly,
Refusing to look,
Trying to deny their existence,
To walk blindly through the maze,
Feeling my way
With my hands
Warm with their blood,
Or was it mine?
Or the blood of men I'd killed?

I continued to grope my way along,
Lost somewhere between reality
And a nightmare that couldn't be real.

I'm still groping my way along,
Still on patrol,
Lost in that world between sleep and wake,
Between nightmare and reality,
Between life and death.

I keep waiting to wake up from the dream,
To find myself in some safe place
With all the guys,
To find out that they
Had been sitting safely in their bunker all this time,
Waiting for me to return from this lonely patrol,
Sitting around laughing at the joke,
At my suffering,
At their sadistic sense of humor.

To have them smile and release me from my imagined debt,
A debt too large to bear,
A debt impossible to pay.

To tell me that I wasn't responsible,
That I wasn't to blame,
That my life wasn't bought with theirs.

That it is simply life,
Short or long,
Good or bad.

There is no debt
Except that which I've created in my own mind.

And it is okay for me to have survived,
It is okay for me to be alive,
And it is okay for me to live,
To stop carrying the burden of their deaths,
To stop punishing myself.

I owe them nothing,
Or everything.

Perhaps that is why I lived,
To tell you this story,
Their story,
The story of their lives,
Their deaths,
Their suffering,
Their sacrifices.

Perhaps the debt is paid.

Part IV

Last Patrol

See To It Yourself

I have killed men.
It took a long time to admit that to myself,
Much less admit it to you.

As a soldier
I have killed,
Out of necessity,
Out of revenge,
Out of rage.

But I lost my spirit,
My soul,
Myself.

So I have put down my gun.
I have emptied my hands.

I walk in peace,
In penance,
Living a life of contrition
For the damage I have done.

I will kill no more.
I want no more of violence.
I have already given you my soul.

If you want more men dead
See to it yourself.

Not through surrogates,
Not from afar,
But up close,
At a few paces
Where you can see their eyes,
Their pain, their fear.

Up close
Where you can taste and smell the effects of your violence,
So you can carry their faces forever
And see their blood on your hands.

If you want more men dead
See to it yourself.

1975

The Resurrection

All these years I thought you were alive,
Or was it my denial that gave you life?

I worked so hard then and through the years
To keep you alive,
That I denied our common past.

I denied the ambush, I denied the gunfire,
I denied the terror, I denied the killing,
I denied the screams, I denied your blood,
I denied your deaths.

You were alive, or was it an illusion?
There must be some mistake,
Why are all your names on the wall?
And where then is my name?

I was so angry
To find you on this granite wall.
You couldn't be here.
You shouldn't be here.

I pounded the wall with my fists,
In my anger
I tried to tear your names from the black granite face
That held you tightly now as I held you then.

I tried to rewrite the history
Of our shared moments of violence and terror,
As though to remove your names
Would somehow give you life.

But there was no resurrection,
Not for you,
But perhaps the beginning of one for me.

Foundations

Our past, the good and the bad
Is the rudder of our future.
It is the foundation on which we are built.

"Let it go, forget it" Some say,
But to deny our past is to deny ourselves.

Holding on to your past, embracing it,
Allows you to grow and learn from it,
To build your future on a strong and honest foundation.

Vietnam is my past,
One of the walls of my foundation,
The good and the bad,
All that I learned
About life, about death,
About love, about friendship,
About hate, about fear,
About ignorance and about arrogance,
But mostly about myself,
It is important to embrace and remember all of it.

It is not all that I am,
But it is part of my foundation,
And part of who I am.

Going Home

I'm going back,
Perhaps I never left,
Am I just going back to pick up myself?
Or to reunite the pieces
And to be where I can be whole?

How many times have I started on this journey?
How many times have I thought about this trip?
Planned it
Only to turn away,
Afraid to go,
Afraid of never coming back,
Or perhaps of being unable to find myself,
Or to find the pieces of myself
Too broken,
Too scattered across the landscape.

But I know I must return,
At least to look,
To make the effort,
To try to find what I lost
Even if I can't define it,
Or am unsure what I'm looking for.

All I know is that it was the last place
I was alive.
It is the place I died.

I at least owe it to myself
To visit my grave,
To bury the pieces,
To mourn the loss.

I'm going back.
I'm going home.

THANH NHÀN
NHÀ THUỐC TƯ NHÂN

Hanoi Memories

There are no air-raid sirens,
Only the wail of horns.

There is no roar of fighter jets,
Only the din of motorbikes.

There is no gun fire,
Only the rattle of Asian voices.

I lay in my bed in downtown Hanoi
Listening to these noises,
Confused by the absence of the war noises I somehow expected.

CNN says nothing of the war,
The war is active only in my mind,
Only in my memory.

Hanoi is at peace in 2001.
Viet Nam is at peace.

It only remains for me to join her.

Pham Thi Yen Nhi

We met by chance in Hue, Vietnam in April 2001,
Perhaps not by chance but by fate,
For it seemed meant to be from the first moments.

She sold me a baguette and touched my life,
There was something about her, in that first moment, that attracted me to her, that made me want to stay and visit,
She had a quiet intelligence, a fierce determination to succeed,
And the bright sparkle of an impish personality behind the serious mask
Fashioned by the lessons of a hard life.
It was one of those immediate connections so rare in life,
The kind that is best accepted rather than thought about or questioned.

In our visits we found a similarity in our thinking,
In our feelings despite our obvious differences.

Our spirits reached across the distance of generations and cultures
And embraced each other,
We felt like family.

We sat along the banks of the Perfume River
Sharing food and our lives,
Opening parts of our souls neither of us had expected to share.

We watched the river and felt the connected currents of our lives,
We talked about life, about cultures,
About families, about war,
About loves and hurts,
About hopes and dreams.

To honor the love and respect we developed for each other
She calls me father. I call her daughter.

We spent the days together as father and daughter,
Knowing we only had a brief time to be in each other's lives,
And wanting to drink it all in, to savor each moment together.

We talked about children and art,
We sat in the parks and played and drew with the children,
I felt the dim coals of my childhood,
And the warmth of the children's joy,
We attended her university classes together and talked with her teachers,
She is the first person from her village to attend the university.

I listened to her teachers talk of her accomplishments,
Proud of her and proud to have her call me father,
Reminded of so many similar meetings with teachers,
With my two daughters in Minnesota in years past.

We rode bikes 35 kilometers to her home village,
Against the protests of some
That thought an old foreigner would die on such a long ride,
But I was used to rides of such distance and made it easily
To be welcomed and embraced by her family.

Her mother hurried to the market place
To gather fixings for a welcoming meal,
While her father told me that he now farmed a small plot
After spending sixteen years in the army of the South.

Just a short walk through the village, we met her uncle
Who spent twenty-five years as a Viet Cong fighter,
On the opposite side from his brother,
I wondered about the tension in the family during those years or even now,
And how Nhi was affected by this history.

Nhi took me to her brother's special place,
We burned incense and left offerings of food,
I felt so honored to share such a special place and personal feelings.

We walked the streets of Hue sharing the years and the memories,
Our hearts entwined if not our hands.

We formed a permanent connection that transcends
Culture, age and gender,
And now distance.

From thousands of miles away we are connected and in touch,
I feel her presence through these memories,
And through her words.

Nhi, my daughter, writes to me:

"Father, today I received the pictures of you in Hue,
Tonight is so special to me I cannot sleep,
My soul is deep in the great joys."

"My heart seems to be broken because of the happiness,
All of a sudden, all the memories about you appear slowly like a film in my mind."

"I'll be the safe-guard of your sleep every night
Until you return to walk the streets of Hue with me again."

"I miss you,
Hue misses you,
The trees miss you,
The river misses you,
The streets miss you,
None of us will be happy until you return."

"Love your daughter, Pham Thi Yen Nhi."

With her words,
With friendship and her love,
This very special Vietnamese woman, wise beyond her years,
Embraced me,
Offering me acceptance, forgiveness and hope.

Knowing her gives me great joy.
I am proud and honored to call her my daughter.